My "Operation Desert Storm"

My suggestion for the
United States 1st Gulf War
(The 100 Hour War)
By
Harvey Carroll, Jr.
"THE UNELECTED PRESIDENT"

Richmond man says he helped organize Panama invasion, war

By Chad Carlton
Herald-Leader staff writer

If what Harvey Carroll Jr. says is to be believed, he is the most influential international political figure in Kentucky.

Among his claims:

• Named and planned "Operation Just Cause," the U.S. military strike that deposed Panamanian dictator Manuel Noriega.

"I told my CIA contact, 'Why don't we go in with low-intensity action to bring him in,'" Carroll said.

• Helped organize the coalition support for "Operation Desert Storm," the war against Iraq.

"I wasn't a Schwarzkopf out there in the desert," he said. "But I do think my suggestions did bring about a quick end to the war."

Harvey Carroll Jr.

Age: 27

Residence: Richmond

This is my fourth book; and a near 30 page Poem on "Desert Storm." Books include a Mini-Autobiography "THE UNELECTED PRSIDENT), SCREWED, which is about the Lewinsky sex scandal and my involvement in Clinton's "Little White House Lie," and my "Operation Just Cause;"my suggestion for the Panama Invasion…

I intend to publish a series of Books under the trademark
"THE UNELECTED PRESIDENT"

ISBN-13:
978-1530032976

ISBN-10:
1530032970

CONTENTS

INTRODUCTION

Far too often in the world of Politics we find that things are not as they appear. We also know that only a hand full of people get credit for successful policy; while, failures are certain to go the other way...

In this book, you will find that President Bush, Sr. Colin Powell, and General Schwarzkopf while deserving became the benefactors of my political analysis that helped to organize and maintain the multinational coalition during the 1st Gulf War "Operation Desert Storm" (The 100 Hour War.)

You will learn that my planning, organizing, strategy on implementation and budgeting saved millions of lives and effected the economic fate of nations. Quite contrary to my warnings not to return to Iraq on unjust bad and/or fabricated intelligence that led to President George W. Bush, VP Dick Cheney, Secretary of Defense Rumsfeld's, and NSA Secretary Condi Rice's return. A return that dilly dallies around in the desert for a decade squandering trillions of dollars. At one time nearly 2.2 billion a day was going to defense, while importing 12 to 18 times less oil per day.

Simply put America's common Defense had lost its commonsense. Vast debt increases as debt was a bit over 4 trillion in 2,000 to just going over 19 trillion. www.usdebtclock.org. This type of mismanagement led to the worst economic downturn since The Great Depression and destabilized not only the Middle East, but the Global Economy....

If you're looking for answers to why, I can't tell you... Probably, money and just pure mismanagement and disrespect for the Office of the President of the United States...

In this book, I show you that there is a problem in the Middle East that is based upon religious, political, and business philosophies that are undermining Civil

Society. We are adding fuel to the fire, which must stop...

This book can be read by nearly anyone that has an interest in the 1st Gulf War, the military, especially those that served in the War. It is also a great read for Diplomats and Military Strategist. But, please try to focus providing constructive leadership...

By reading the book you will get a fast pace view of how juggling time, and what is in a number of people's minds and various avenues that can be taken to affect policy. Yet, seeing what most can't via sound bites that lead to successful big picture conclusions...

I can assure you that it is not easy. Some have a unique ability. Mine is sleep apnea, and a love of politics. I rarely sleep; therefore, I spend double and/or triple the time that others would. Praying for wisdom certainly doesn't hurt either... And you must convince yourself that you can lead, because if you fall, an entire country can fall with you... So, learning to eat stress for breakfast, lunch and dinner is required. But, you have to find ways to make obstacles much smaller.

Carry a marble representing the World on your Key Chain might work... Helped me... Its better than thinking you have the weight of the World on your shoulders...

Oh, and did I mention praying... Oh, and don't forget to pray... ;-)

DEDICATION

This book is dedicated to those working with The United Nations and Global Citize3ns that work daily paid and unpaid to help develop constructive policy leadership, and it is also dedicated to the millions of displaced people from the countries discussed within this book.

1

ME AND THE UNITED NATIONS "REPUTATION AND CREDIBILITY"

Reputation and credibility are key character traits that increase the effectiveness of carrying out economic statecraft and/or any political policy; be that policy local, state, national or international.

Reputation and Credibility issues have haunted me from day one that I began participating in the political arena. In fact, most of my life's quest has been to establish either my reputation or credibility. Even after establishment, there is always going to be someone that will try to diminish your character and integrity and twist your reputation and credibility for their own purpose, especially the "<u>negative by nature press</u>".

Reputation and Credibility are concepts character traits that are interrelated when it comes to establishing a perception of power and influencing policy. It is a must have for a public figure to have in order to establish themselves publically and maintain confidence and sound policy...

I would advise **policy-makers** *to be very aware of what they say and how well they follow through. No* **policy-maker** *wants to get a reputation as a "bull-shitter" who does not back up what they say. Especially when dealing with any Military option. Military options are always on the table in high-level politics, and you will see throughout this book that I have advised using them more than once.*

However, one must have patients and faith that other options can be carried out instead of a military option, because military options are costly in the loss of lives, as well as economically; therefore, it must be used only as a last resort when Diplomacy has failed, failed, failed and failed again... Even after they have exhausted all talks, then people can come together under their faith in God, and see their commonalities and best wishes for others as they see their wishes for themselves and their own families and friends...

The first step is to foster Democracy, focus on the Declaration of Human Rights along with a sound Diplomacy Policy of Economic Development; using a hand-up, instead of a hand-out approach.

Such Development and Diplomacy can be carried out more affectively by the use of technical "Comprehensive Development Tools than providing money. Such Economic Statecraft tools can be a tool used at both the International Policy Level as well as within each American City within the United States.

I am not an isolationist, I am an Internationalist and I strongly believe that America has a role to play in the World. As long as those policies are helping America provide economic growth that helps improve GDP, which can fund, and build new quality housing, roads/rail, create millions of jobs, and educate our citizens.

I am certain that America's role should be more as a mentor instead of a militant. This starts by realizing that the Military has over two-million under their control, and only about six-thousand Diplomats.

With this vast inequality in the Department of State and the Department of Commerce, it is no wonder that America is the number one exporter of War and Weaponry in the

World, and that there is a lack of peace within the world.

Comprehensive Planning should be shared with each and every Foreign City in need of USAID and willing to appreciate and embrace the value of ethical Capitalism, Diplomacy and Development.

I highly suggest that the Department of State and the Department of Commerce become more closely related and section off a portion of the Military such as the Corp of Engineers, Merchant Marines and other key groups to focus on growth and development, and enhancing International Commerce.

These groups should be used to focus on international investments, and development to build communities and nations, while expanding trade and commerce. This will bring jobs back to Wall Street and Main Street America and *provide security for the capital markets and grow exports from America which now has a trade imbalance of over 1 Trillion Dollars a year when you add in Oil Imports...*

New and innovative Trade and Commerce must not be special interest in nature as the treasury draining aspects of War. John Perkins states that many nations in the past have been duped out of their money via Defense contractors and shadow banks in his book "Confessions of an Economic Hit Man"[1]. It fact, Perkins states that it was his job to package and sell a false bill of goods that robbed treasuries... I say to you that our beloved Uncle Sam has fallen victim of an Economic Hit Man...

"The Department of National and International Development and Diplomacy" should be an overall

---

[1] ". http://www.economichitman.com "Confessions of an Economic Hitman" by John Perkins

acceptable plan where it does not negatively affect the American economy, and/or disrupt it as we have seen with two wars in Afghanistan and Iraq.

For nearly a decade the lion's share of American Tax Dollars went to fund the "Beltway Bandits" from within Washington, D.C... The false bill of goods sold to the American people ramped up Defense spending from just over 300 Billion a year to triple with overseas contingencies to the near 900 Billion a year...

Nearly a Trillion a year spent for nearly a decade on wars of choice as opposed to necessities... I can make this statement as I advised the win of the 1st *Gulf War in 37 Days as opposed to decade of dilly dallying around spending Trillions and costing America more than 16 Trillion in Economic losses, tripling the American National Debt from nearly 5 Trillion to a nearly 15 Trillion Dollars...*

The Department of National and International Development and Commerce" should continue to have a separation of powers falling under the Executive Branch with Congressional Approved Office Heads and/or the President appoints special Diplomatic Representatives to deal with International Conflict resolution, and countries that could lead to conflict. We have too much of a focus on "Death Democracy" as opposed to economic growth and development...

The Chief Diplomat via the State Department wing and/or appointed special representative should still focus on economic statecraft tools of Diplomacy, International Trade and Commerce tools such as those addressed by Jonathan Kirshner[2] related to "Sanctions."

---

[2] Jonathan Kirshner, "The Micrfoundations of Economic Sanctions," <u>Security Studies</u>, Vol. 6, No. 3 (Spring, 1997), pp. 32-64.

Perhaps I will discuss in another book about Iran, Sanctions and Security.... I'm not sure, but perhaps, because I too spent a great deal of time writing on both Iranian and Russian Sanctions, the possible outcomes...

2
MY SYNDICATION OF DESERT STORM

*The August 1990 Iraqi invasion and occupation of Kuwait sparked an international response. The end result was a war in the Persian Gulf, better known as "Operation Desert Shield and later upgraded to Desert Storm". This left many Americans asking did the "**End Justify the Means**". For me that was never a question. I supported the US 100%.*

*Many people throughout this nation and others just didn't have a clue as to why the war started, much less the common sense to logically evaluate the "**Risk-vs.-The Rewards**" of fighting for **Kuwait**. This includes the American military that originally opposed any action. Yet, the way it was handled to keep the profiteers out was key as well. The intelligence or the "thinking" was* *beyond citizens and corporations ability to understand. The issues were just too complex as I mentioned from the class I took in 1985.*

The largest problem is simply people are poorly educated or really don't care about international affairs. To get to the point I will cut out the history of Iraq and the fact that Kuwait was valuable to our national interest and go straight into the story.

*The United States Congress was a lot smarter than one would give credit to. Congress recognized the need to protect the flow of oil. This was clearly acknowledged when **The US Congress voted to re-flag Kuwaiti ships starting in 1987.***

In my opinion reflagging ships was a very reasonable policy that sent a warning that any interference with Kuwaiti oil exports would be considered an act of aggression against the US and its interest. It didn't get any clearer than that. This to me also meant that Kuwait as a country should be safe from aggression. After all there are a lot of U.S. and U.N. investments in that region, particularly in Kuwait.

Finally, in the late 80's when the Iran/Iraq war had ceased and everything seemed to be relatively calm in the Middle East. Suddenly in August 1990 without any public warning, Iraq's President Saddam Hussein ordered a violent invasion of Kuwait.

This is where I got personally involved. To get to the point, I called the Intelligence Analyst up several times, sometimes collect and several times from my office where I worked as a real estate sales associate in Richmond, KY.

Our conversations consisted of me sharing my thoughts of what I had studied about the Middle East during old International Relations and US Foreign Policy Classes. I shared the following:

- *I shared basic religious, political and business philosophies of the region.*

- *I felt that perhaps my suggestions may overt a war or at least buy some time to prepare for a war.*

- *I openly shared some half-baked ideas that President Bush could do or say that would sell his actions or create rumors that would buy some time.*

- *One such rumor was to get the word out that Kuwait was side drilling and stealing Iraqi oil.*

- *Reminded them that our strongest partner in the area would be Saudi Arabia and that they would most likely go along with anything we wished.*

In response to the invasion, President bush sent 260,000 troops to one of our strongest business partners in the Middle East; Saudi Arabia. The U.S. troops began to dig in at the border of Saudi to set up a security zone to protect the Saudis from any further expansion intentions of Iraq. Simultaneously, the rumor of side drilling began to circulate.

I made the suggestion mainly because I had studied under Command Sgt. Major Harrison in my (International Relations and US Foreign Policies Class in 1985, while taking classes at Central Texas College (European Campus) while in the Army.

3
"INTERNATIONAL RELATIONS AND U.S. FOREIGN POLICY" PREVENTING WWIII
(The first time)

Class with Command Sgt. Major Harrison. Harrison was an instructor for my International Relations and U.S. Foreign Policy class through Central Texas College, (European Campus) in Baumholder, West Germany during my Army assignment in 1985/6.

*Harrison painted the picture of WWIII being started in the Persian Gulf over the vast oil reserves. **He stated it was up to us to prevent it...***

Like a lighting strike, I felt that calling... Seriously, I really felt as if I had been tasked to do just that; Prevent WWIII from occurring. sure, I was a young Army kid, but this higher calling and purpose was almost a glimpse of the future...

By reflecting back on the class discussions of how things might unfold, who is friend and foe, who believes this or that philosophy of religion, business and politically.

Basically, getting into the mindset of the countries of the Middle East, the World and then as leadership changed, get into their minds...

Being aware of this and conducting additional research on what if's I found myself ready when the time arose... Look, I didn't sit around thinking about Armageddon and the like. It was just a class of probabilities. Those probabilities came to pass and I just happened to have contacts that could shape the outcome...

My forward thinking made me realize that any conflict in the area could get out of hand very easily. Thereby, costing millions of lives and affecting the economic fate of many nations.

With this in mind I began to think of ways to avoid a destructive ends and WWIII/Armageddon actually starting.

Before I go much further, I want to ensure that you realize what the US was up against. Or could have been up against if sound/decisive diplomacy hadn't been used.

This was the difficulties in Diplomacy that I had somewhat seen in my mind's eye many years before in my "International Relations and U.S. Foreign Policy" classes.

THESE ARE MAJOR MIDDLE EASTER PLAYERS[3]

Egypt	*2.3 Million*
Israel	*5.3 West Bank*
	1.6 and Gaza 0.7
* Saudi Arabia	*17.5*
Jordan	*3.8*
Lebanon	*3.6*
Syria	*13.5*
* UAE	*2.1*
* Kuwait	*1.7*
* Iraq	*19.2*
* Iran	*62.8 Million*
* Libya	*4.9*
Turkey	*60.7*

---

[3] CIA=The World Fact book 1992, Washington, D. C.: Central Intelligence Agency, 1992. PRB= Population Reference bureau, 1993 WORLD POPULATION DATA SHEET, Washington, D.C., 1993.

Also note, (*) represents OPEC nations. OPEC stands for organization of Petroleum Exporting Countries, which was formed in 1960 by eleven nations; seven of them were Arab nations that controlled the market. They set prices by controlling production in 1973 they increased prices 4 times the index price.

Adding Iraq, Iran, Libya, Syria, Lebanon and Jordan which are countries that just didn't care to much for the United States.

A total of 107.8 Million Arabs that could have easily opposed us making Vietnam look like a walk in the park.

- *To prevent this from happening, I suggested that President Bush bypass Congress and go directly to the United Nations to organize a coalition.*

- *I mentioned that it is easier to sell people on human rights than it would be on defending oil. I thought of some of our old marching songs while in Basic Training which had words to the effect of "rape, kill, pillage and burn-eat babies".*

- *I know it isn't a pleasant thought but the idea was to prepare new troops for the horrors of war. Perhaps the phrases came out of the resentment from the Vietnam War where our American Servicemen had been called baby killers. Anyway, with such horrific thought in mind I could only imagine what the Iraqi soldiers were doing to the Kuwait Citizens, therefore I made the following suggestions:*

  o *Therefore, I felt that it was best to condemn the Naked Act Of Aggression" by selling the American people on the explicit violations of "Human Rights".*

President Bush used the statements effectively to set the stage for our opposition to Iraq's invasion.

Before I get into the technical and/or strategic aspects of the war I would like to share a bit of research with you. To grasp the reality of death and excessive waste of money that exist in war here are some destructive statistics:[4]

A. Major Nations Battle deaths of

	_WW I_	**_W W II_**
United States	116,516	405,399
Great Britain	908,000	357,116
Russia USSR	1,800,000	6,115,000
France	1,357,800	201,568
Germany	1,773,700	3,250,000
Japan		1,270,000
China		1,324,000

B. Estimated costs of War to U.S. in $ Dollars.

Revolutionary War	158,000
Civil War	13,000,000
World War I	112,000,000
World War II	664,000,000
Vietnam	140,800,000,000

---

[4] Obtained from Dr. Cecil Orchard of Eastern Kentucky University during an early undergrad class.

Total cost of WWII has been estimated to be 1,500,000,000,000. An estimate at the end of the Gulf War was a cost of 70 Billion and about 150,000 lives Iraqi lives lost, with less than 500 American/Allies.

Huntington[5] refers to the syndication of "Desert Storm" as "Tin Cup Diplomacy". In a way it was; however, I liked to look at it as being one of the largest syndicated real estate deals ever.

Years later in 1999 during my own Presidential run I mentioned that to Donald Trump associates, which considered me as a potential Trump Vice Presidential Candidate[6].

---

[5] Samuel P. Huntington, "The Erosion of American National Interest. (25th Anniversary Issue)" Foreign Affairs v76, n5 (Sept-Oct 1997): 28-40.

[6] Donald Trump for President Committee, "Letter discussing potential VP running mate position".

December 14, 1999

Harvey Carroll, Jr.
806 Brockton
Richmond, KY 40475

Dear Mr. Carroll,

Mr. Trump appreciates your offer to join him as the Vice Presidential candidate in the 2000 election. Currently, he is seriously considering a bid for the Reform Party Presidential nomination and will make a decision early next year. Since he is not a declared candidate for the Presidency at this time, it is simply too early for him to consider possible running mates.

He believes the Republicans have gone too far to the Right. The Democrats have gone too far to the Left. Mr. Trump thinks the Reform Party could offer the citizens of our country the best opportunity to address the needs of the working men and women in the center.

It is time for the United States to have a leader who can break the logjam in Washington. Americans need that leader to negotiate real tax relief and reform our healthcare, social security and campaign finance systems.

Mr. Trump agrees with you that our next President must be someone who sees the big picture and is not beholden to special interests. Perhaps America is ready to have an experienced businessman who will run America like a business at the helm.

Your support is greatly appreciated.

Sincerely,

Roger Stone, Director
Donald J. Trump Presidential Exploratory Committee

Trump Tower   725 Fifth Avenue   15th Floor   New York, NY 10022   212.688.7230 (TEL)   212.688.4020 (FAX)
www.Donald-JTrump2000.com

I'm not sure that Trump's ego could have stood the competition, but perhaps as a businessman he would have appreciated the sound business perspective of syndicating a deal that cost the U.S. very little, with great gains. A deal that did not allowing profiteers to destroy our nation and force a major economic downturn and stealing the American Dream...

Many felt that it was bad that Germany and Japan had trouble coming up with their share of the money to finance the war; however, we have to cut them some slack and realize that Germany was going through the high cost of reunification and Japan was entering a recession. In addition, The United States at the time at more outflow than inflow revenues. There weren't the 100 plus billion dollar surpluses that we have seen after President Clinton was elected.

Psychological operations began by making it look like we may consider giving Kuwait to Iraq by starting rumors that Kuwait was stealing oil from Iraq via "Side Drilling". This rumor, along with setting a six-month deadline gave Saddam some security and peace of mind. It allowed him to think that the

United States would not be willing to pay a price to regain Kuwait.

I would assume that Saddam felt that Kuwait was money in the bank; however, he wanted to ensure that that money was in a well-secured bank. So, Saddam's army built fire trenches, heavily land mined the area and took many other tactical precautions of any assault. Saddam know that there would be a very, very high price to pay for any assault on his entrenched army.

- *I also made suggestions to start rumors that some of Saddam's top military aids tried to assassinate him. Hoping that they would and end the thing without a war. He countered by publicly executing those who he felt could be in any way shape or from disloyal to him. So much for that rumor...*

Saddam was playing the same propaganda or psychological operations game we were. He too was trying to organize a coalition. His coalition would of course counter any American Imperialists influence on the Arab Nations.

4
OUT THINKING, PLANNING AND ORGANIZING SADDAM HUSSEIN

I anticipated Saddam's thoughts long before he thought them. "Granted I'm looking at this lightly; however, I give Saddam credit for being a great strategist (General Schwarzkopf at the end of the war said Saddam wasn't much of a strategist; however, I disagree. Saddam was an excellent strategist. We were just a bit faster on the draw.)"

To counter the primary attempt that Saddam would, and did use to build his own coalition we needed to isolate him from any friends. I felt that President Bush should vocalize to the world the following statements:

- *"It's not just the United States against Saddam Hussein; it's the entire world against Saddam Hussein".*

I think that by establishing relations with neighboring countries of Iraq it created a state of paranoia for Saddam. Not knowing the future of his country and having the feeling that the walls could just close in on him at anytime.

This even included a classified deal with the former Soviet Union/Russian President Gorbachev. *I think that the deal was cut at the Helsinki Summit. All I know is that I put the words in Gorbachev's mouth.*

• *The key to organizing the coalition and keeping it together was to influence Israel to stay out of the conflict entirely.*

• *When the war started that became an even harder thing to do. Israel became Saddam's trump card trying to use it to divide the coalition. If used properly Saddam know that he could almost instantly gain over 107.8 million coalitions that could envelop the United States and its allies in the region.*

Israel knew that if they participated, Jordan would retaliate because they had warned Israel not to use their air space. Granted King Hussein of Jordan was a peacemaker; however, he was a politician at heart and his people had a great deal of animosity against Israel.

*The real problem was the **"Armageddon line of thinking".** Any type of conflict between Israel and one of its neighbors would cause the U.S. to be aligned with them directly.*

The Christians in the United States were already thinking that we should just team up with Israel and go have an all out Armageddon like war of biblical proportion.

Yet, I always felt that God would not want us to blow the world up or even a 1/3rd of it, which contained the Middle Eastern tyrant Saddam Hussein. Therefore, we had to be proactive and do everything possible to maintain the coalition and keep effort by Saddam to wedge the coalition from happening.

A very destructive war could have happened if it were not for sound diplomacy. If we had participated with Israel it would have become strategically necessary to "Nuke" the swarming troops.

Just in case the conflict got out of hand I sort of anticipated that a Nuclear Sub was in the area somewhere and it may be needed and I knew how to use them. I had taken a two-week course while in the military that taught me what NBC (Nuclear, Biological, and Chemical) weapons could do and how they might be used.

I realized that a few well-placed Nukes' could take care of any mass aggression directed towards Israel and/or the security forces deployed to the region.

Yet, I felt that if a nuke hit the oil and gas that a 1/3rd of the Earth could be blown out into space. It might be nice to have a second moon, but didn't feel nuking the area would be the best idea. That is why I'm for a "Nuclear Free Middle East." Anyway, to maintain overall control and prevent mass destruction I recommended additional strategies:

- *Temporary become aligned and do business dealings with Syria (Whom had been considered a terrorist nation) and allow them to become part of the coalition.*

    o *Coincidentally the Pan Am. bombing was diverted from*

being Syria's responsibility to being blamed Libya.

o *Just so happens that the F.B.I. Agent that found the linking evidence was from Richmond, Kentucky and made the news paper discussing the topic at the time.*

• *A classified deal with Russia (After all Middle East was in the Soviet Union's hemisphere and deployment forces are only about 300 miles away from Iraq) as a last minute plea to influence Iraq to back out of Kuwait.*

o *Requested to have the Soviet Union to publicly state that they would "guarantee Iraq's borders" if they would back out of Kuwait.*

o *I assume that the diplomacy negotiation between the United*

States and Gorbachev occurred during the Helsinki Summit.

While President Bush was out playing golf and fishing I was in Richmond, KY being a barfly with the weight of the world on my shoulders.

I realize that it is bad to drink and such. I justified it as I felt that I needed to get trashed to relieve some of the ultimate stress.

As my six-month deadline date was quickly approaching. The final days it became important to set aside Bushes wimp factor and hype up the media and mentally prepare the troops for conflict.

I called up with some additional quotes/rumors. I wanted to ensure people realized that we were up against, i.e. a million man army.

- *"The 4th largest army in the world"*

- "It's not going to be another Vietnam" "Saddam isn't going against 15 year olds with sticks and stones she will be going up against highly motivated and highly trained military personal with the best weapons and equipment money can buy"

- "Saddam is a ruthless dictator that plunged his country into a bloody eight year war with Iran".

- "Saddam even used chemical weapons of mass destruction against his own people",

    o And of course even comparing the guy to "Hitler".

- I even silly stuff to watch President Bush say it to give me the added confidence I needed to continue my focus.

o   *I recommended mentioning MC Hammer "Drop the Hammer on him". Soldiers identified with the point during Bush's visit to the Desert. It sort of psychological prepared the soldiers to be prepared to "drop the hammer", or to be prepared to shoot the enemy.*

•   *In the final hours it was hyped up like the "Show Down at the O.K. Coral" one of my favorite Westerns of all time. My dad and I had watched many versions of the Western on T.V. and it always has some intensity leading up to the deadline.*

5
HOLDING THE
MULTINATIONAL COALITION
TOGETER

I had anticipated Saddam Hussein trying to involve Israel to break up the multinational coalition. I had asked the Bush Administration to ask Israel to be prepared and to stay out of the 1st Gulf War.

- *I continued to make sure that Israel kept out of the war even though scud missiles from Iraq were being used against them.*

   ○ *Strategy wise, I also felt that it was not smart to participate in any type of ground war, because a long-term conflict would cause the coalition to break up.*

   ○ *I realized that nearly 150,000 of Iraq's top troops (The*

Republican Guards) were entrenched in the Oil Fields of Kuwait with oil trench fires, machine gun and such nest on top of buildings and oil refineries. They could pose a slaughter situation for the Marines if they were to do a frontal assault...

o   *Therefore, I suggested that we blow up the oil fields and the 150,000 Iraqi troops and call it a day, but not without serious praying and asking God if I would lose my soul...*

A prayer that led me to make a case that such action would save millions of lives and affect the economic fate of nations... I wrote a poem on this "Prayer Chat with God" that you may be interested in reading...

- *Oil fires-- I felt that it was basically it is Saddam's fault, because he started the war and he would was destroying a number of oil wells. Therefore, he should be blamed for the "environmental terrorism" even if the U.S. blew the hell out of the oil fields as a strategic move to destroy the mass of Republican Guards.*

- *I also started rumors that some of Iraq's pilot's had defected to Iran. This kept the Joint Chiefs/military on their toes.   Made them aware of another potential threat and forced them to keep track of what Iran was up to.*

If you remember, Iran didn't like us very much either.   Iran after all had labeled us "The Great Satan" during our previous political encounters.   Because of the hate Iran had for America, I felt that Iran could have fairly easily participated with Iraq even though they had been at war with Iraq for over Eight years.

So, I started a rumor that some of their piolets had defected. Just to get the military realizing that they had to cover their flank... And to make Iran realize that if their pilots were to come into the theater of war that they would not be returning...

6
EXIT STRATEGY
SELLING SCHWARTZKOPF ON
(THE 100 HOIUR WAR)

Yet the most compelling thing that still haunts me is the decision of General Schwarzkopf, which made the decision to do a "Hale Mary Play" and send troops into areas where they would be attacked by nerve gas. I didn't think that he needed to do a Hale Mary. Especially when you are winning the war!

Also General Schwarzkopf should have known from day one that a long term conflict would have caused the coalition to fall apart; thereby, turning 107.8 million Arabs against our efforts.

As I mentioned earlier poor strategic decisions could have turned Desert Storm into a war environment where the United States and its allies could be swarmed by the other Arab states and put Russia and China into positions whereby they would become profiteers quest for a market to sell weapons to the opposing forces.

A Ground War was a very poor judgment on General Schwarzkopf's part. The General ignored the warning and/or had no intentions of stopping according to quotes I read from "The Generals War[7]". If such an approach was deliberate on Schwarzkopf's behalf, then, I feel that Schwarzkopf and he alone was responsible for our troops that got affected by nerve gas.

The troops should not have been placed in that situation when we could have continued to use air strikes to weaken the threats. It was made clear by President Bush, that if weapons of mass destruction were used then the United States would have reacted accordingly.

---

[7] Michael R. Gordon and General Bernard E. Trainor: <u>The Generals' War: The Inside Story of the Conflict in the Gulf</u>. Little, Brown and Company Boston, NY, Toronto, London.

I know, because I wrote that statement also. I think we would have retaliated with weapons of mass destruction ourselves, which would have most likely wiped Baghdad off the face of the earth.

Next, there are many people who think that we should have just stayed out of the war and let Iraq have Kuwait. I say those people are week minded and were not mentally prepared to analyze and make the tough decisions that would be required to accomplish the mission. That included the military most of the Generals involved[8]; however, I do have some respect for General Michael Dugan[9] that broke ranks and made similar suggestions of bombing the entrenched Iraqi troops, even though I

---

[8] Dr. Michael C. Desch, Civilian Control of the Military: The Changing Security Environment (Baltimore: The Johns Hopkins University Press, 1999), pg. 31.
[9] Dr. Michael C. Desch, Civilian Control of the Military: The Changing Security Environment (Baltimore: The Johns Hopkins University Press, 1999), pg. 31.

had already discussed that strategy long before he did.

Many say that the US entered the war for political reasons to improve the popular image of President Bush. I'll be the first to tell you that's a bunch of bullshit. President Bush handled the matter in a just and caring way.

In my opinion he was very economically aware of the US and its interest abroad. Without his leadership abilities in defending Kuwait this country would have felt a severe economic downturn not to mention the thought of losing a lot of lives.

I feel for our combat veterans. I feel that they deserve much better treatment than they received after the Gulf War. I'm truly sorry that lives that were lost; however, I realize that it could have been much, much worse.

I have told myself many times that "The End Justified The Means" and to be honest there probably hasn't been a day that has passed since the Gulf War that I haven't thought about it. Yet, I just keep telling myself that I saved millions of lives and had a very positive effect on the economic fate of this Nation...

I would like to make a bit of a political statement and remind people that it doesn't take a mental heavy weight to realize that our oil/fuel dependency problem needs to be looked at in respect to long-range economic security.

Hopefully, we can come up with some quick solutions, such as electric cars, especially for the larger cites. Perhaps give huge tax incentives to the oil and gas companies to invest with the auto manufactures.

For instance, General Motors Corvette plant in Kentucky could be converted into an electric car producer if the incentives for investment were created. We also need to focus more on mass transit systems and regional industrial development like the Europeans and the Japanese. They have both, industry great mass transit systems.

In fact the European Rail system is state of the art and should be used as a model in this country, especially, now that we live in a post 911 world. We need to start developing regional World Trade Centers along Americas Railways instead of having one World Trade Center that is an easy target.

The rest is history. We basically won the war in the Gulf in 37 days.

7
TWO STATE SOLUTIONS VIA A PALISTIN STATE AGAINST A RETURN TO WAR IN IRAQ

In 1999 I was completing my Bachelors of Business Administration and had decided to voice my concerns about the political climate.

I saw then Governor Bush starting to ramp up a lot of Neo-Conservative comments that sort of scared me with his Middle Eastern policy views. He appeared to be getting on the go back to the Middle East band wagon. This concerned me a great deal.

I thought it important to take the time to write him with my offer to provide sound intelligence of the complex issue as to the Justification why his father did not go to Baghdad.

I hoped that he would also listen to reason as his father did.

Governor/Presidential Candidate Bush sent me the following letter for my EKU graduation.

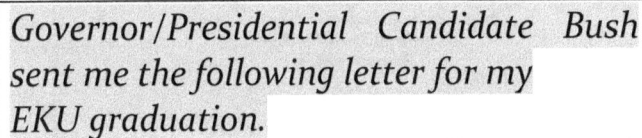

STATE OF TEXAS
OFFICE OF THE GOVERNOR

GEORGE W. BUSH
GOVERNOR

November 30, 1999

Greetings to:

Harvey Carroll Jr.

Congratulations on your December 11 graduation from Eastern Kentucky University. Completing your college education is a wonderful accomplishment, and I know you and your family are proud.

New challenges await you, and I wish you every success in the future. I encourage you to continue to read and learn because the quest for knowledge can last a lifetime. I hope you will continue to set high goals and work hard to achieve them.

Laura joins me in sending best wishes on this special occasion. God bless you.

Sincerely,

GEORGE W. BUSH

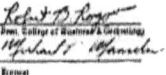

Keep in mind that I am back in school, but I'm watching policy discussions that I think are going towards a radical ends. So, I decided to jump into the Presidential Race.

I was actually a candidate when I wrote Governor/Candidate Bush feeling that he would most likely win, but I was trying to establish a line of credibility and show a background of providing sound advice to his father and other Presidents.

The following are articles related to me running for President on the Reform Party ticket, and 6th Congressional District race years before:

Student enters presidential race

By ANDREW KERSEY
Staff Writer

Harvey Carroll, Jr., of Estill County, is going to run for president. He's not running for Eastern's student body president and he's not trying to become leader of the local Lions Club either. He wants to be the president of the United States.

Carroll, 35, is ready to take his chances on the Reform Party ballot. He hasn't filed the necessary Federal Election Commission paperwork to register for candidacy yet, but says he has them and they will be submitted in time.

Carroll plans to graduate from Eastern after the fall semester with a degree in finance and real estate.

Seeking a career in politics is nothing new for Carroll. He ran for state representative in 1988 and for Estill County judge-executive in 1989. Although he lost both races, he says he has what it takes to lead the country into the next millennium.

The Reform Party is the party that Ross Perot represented in the 1992 presidential election, and the same

> **I think the way Jesse (Ventura) won was very bizarre; he got the wrong notoriety because he was already famous.**
>
> *Harvey Carroll, Jr.,*
> *Eastern student*

party that former professional wrestler Jesse "The Body" Ventura led to the governorship of Minnesota.

When asked if Carroll was inspired by Ventura's success he said, "I think the way Jesse won was very bizarre; he got the wrong notoriety because he was already famous."

Carroll appears to be an average guy with some knowledge about busi-

news and politics. He speaks with a slow southern drawl and exhibits a southern hospitality that is synonymous with young, hopeful politicians without a lot of experience.

While in the Army, he took foreign policy classes through Central Texas College which led to his serious interest in politics, Carroll said.

Carroll believes he has the experience and the financial know-how to be a major political figure in America. Carroll said before he joined the Reform Party he was both a Democrat and a Republican.

"I don't think the Republicans' budget plan will work, and the Reform Party was based on sound economic and business principles," Carroll said when asked what caused him to abandon his previous parties and migrate to the Reform Party.

One other reason Carroll wants to run for president is to take votes away from potential Reform Party candidate

See **Election/A7**

Andrea Brown/Progress

Harvey Carroll, Jr., a senior finance and real estate major from Estill County, is trying to run for president of the United States

Election: not Carroll's first run for office

from the **front**

Pat Buchanan.

Carroll does, however, support possible Reform Party candidate Donald Trump.

Carroll said he had a lot of influence on Presidents Bush and Clinton and former Kentucky Governor Wallace Wilkinson. Carroll claims he has been making policy and pulling strings

from Estill and Madison County since he was in his 20s.

He said he has CIA contacts that relay his messages to important political figures.

He also said he helped organize the coalition support for Operation Desert Storm when the U.S. declared war on Iraq. He said he was a strong influence on George Bush's economic recovery plans.

Carroll's father, Harvey Carroll, Sr., said his son had mentioned his candidacy to him. Carroll, Sr., said he couldn't confirm any of his son's alleged Washington contacts.

What type of president does Carroll, Sr. think his son would make?

"I'd say he'd be as good as what we got," Carroll Sr. said, "Look at what we've got now."

Photo by Fox News

Still not sold? Consider pulling the lever for Harvey Carroll Jr., who totes around a campaign sign painted by his brother and hands out business cards on photocopy paper. He ran for the state legislature as a Democrat but became a Republican during the Bush years because, he believes, he was secretly directing Bush's foreign policy by faxing advice to the CIA and the State Department. "I actually put words in both Bush's and Gorbachev's mouths," he says, then hesitates. "This is sort of classified. If you can water it down, that's cool."

course feels like *The Third Man* bar in post-World War II Vienna—nobody's quite sure who the other guy is working for. Every couple of feet, there's another clipboard with some petitioner trying to draft Ralph Nader or David Boren or Colin Powell.

There are official contenders for the presidential nomination, too, though you haven't heard of them—yet. Harvey Powell, a 34-year-old Kentucky real-estate broker has declared for president. He's still not of age, but that doesn't mean he's shy of experience. Harvey says he's done consulting work for Clinton, helped maintain a multinational coalition against Saddam Hussein, and, through a covert fax system he worked out with a Secret Service agent, controlled nearly everything George Bush said during his presidency. "I had him saying silly stuff during the Gulf War," Harvey confides, "just to ensure that I was still pulling the strings."

But the biggest mystery of the convention is the candidacy of Donald Trump. After a cryptic statement from Trump seeming to deny that he was running, the *New York Times* reported that Trump had pulled the plug on his potential candidacy. But somebody in Dearborn isn't taking him at his word. Everywhere you look in the hotel, you see The Donald's albino-caterpillar eyebrows and the hair that looks like an abandoned nest. Trump is not here in person, but slick Trump 2000 posters were apparently put up by two different sets of Reformers who say they are acting of their own accord, though they both throw parties in posh hospitality suites featuring open bars.

Russ Verney, who is stepping down as chairman of the Reform party after choosing not to run for reelection, smells a rat, or, more precisely, a short-fingered Vulgarian, as *Spy* magazine used to call The Donald. In fact, rumors persist all weekend that covert forces are pushing the candidacy even though Trump himself says he's not running.

It's easy to dismiss Verney as paranoid since he works for Perot, a man convinced that Vietnamese-backed assassins showed up on his front lawn in Dallas. But sources close to one of the Trump 2000 draft groups say that Roger Stone, the former political consultant who does consulting work for Trump on his business deals, is working behind the scenes with some associates to rally support for The Donald. According to several sources, William von Raab, U.S. customs commissioner under Ronald Reagan, and

Dominic Del Papa, a consultant, are pushing a Trump candidacy.

Though von Raab does not return calls seeking comment, I bump into Del Papa at the convention. He tells me the suggestion is ridiculous. Neither he nor von Raab, with whom he works, is supporting Donald Trump. As evidence, he hands me a draft Buchanan for president press release with von Raab's name on it (von Raab was a co-chair in Buchanan's '92 campaign). I ask Del Papa where he can be reached, and he gives me a cellphone number with no company affiliation. "It's just myself," he says, though he says he's worked with Stone before. When I call the Icon public relations firm where Stone works, the receptionist tells me that both von Raab and Del Papa have numbers at the firm.

Stone says the charges that he's behind the Trump groundswell are ridiculous. "Paranoia seems to run rampant [in the Reform Party]," says Stone. "Russ Verney has lost control of his party." Yes,

52

So, you can see I was out on the campaign trail a little, but my priority was to finish my college degree and go to Masters School.

A focus on attending The University of Kentucky's prestigious Patterson School of Diplomacy and International Commerce which I did for a few classes later in 2000/1 school year. Here is a copy of my Student ID.

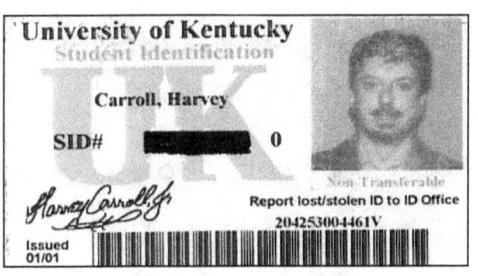

Here is a copy of press from the Lexington Herald Leader, citing me as "The most influential international political future in Kentucky" and the Richmond Register giving me a forum to defend my claims after a very negative article...

NOTE: I knew I had little chance to with running against the former Lexington Mayor; however, I felt it time to begin establishing a public profile for past experiences to be more credible in the future.

Candidate defends claims

By RANDY PATRICK
Register Staff Writer

Harvey Carroll Jr., a Democratic candidate for Congress, yesterday defended his claims that he was involved in planning the United States' last two wars, but offered no evidence to support them.

Speaking to an audience of one reporter at City Hall, Carroll criticized The Richmond Register for publishing a story on April 5 that questioned many of his claims, including those concerning U.S. military operations in Panama and the Persian Gulf. His speech was shown on local public access cable television.

The 27-year-old former military policeman said he influenced national policy through a CIA analyst whom he met while working for an international security agency in New York.

While having dinner and Bible study with the man at his home, Carroll said, he suggested that the U.S. depose Panamanian dictator Manuel Noriega by going in "with low-intensity conflict," capturing him and bringing him to the United States to stand trial on drug charges.

He said it would be similar to the way an automobile dealer was "busted" in his hometown for money laundering in connection with an illegal drug operation.

After Iraq invaded Kuwait in 1990, said Carroll, he called his contact collect to share with him his knowledge of Middle Eastern culture and politics. He said he suggested that President Bush forge a multinational coalition to isolate Iraq, persuade the

HARVEY CARROLL JR.

U.S.S.R. and Israel to stay out of the conflict, and become temporarily allied with Syria. He said he hoped to be able to avert a war, but his plan didn't work.

Note by now I have a BBA and 3 partial masters degrees specializing in

Business, Masters work in Public Administration, Masters work in Diplomacy and International Commerce, in addition I've directly and indirectly advised the past 3 presidents of the United and put words in the mouth of foreign heads of state. So, I sort of had a good grasp on International Relations and U.S. Foreign Policy...

Now to get to the point I had recognized for years the need for the acceptance of Palestinian State. I felt it a key to Middle Eastern Peace and Prosperity.

After 9/11 I voiced my concern for the recognition of a Palestinian State. This did two things. It opened the option to real peace negotiations and it allowed for the listing of a target list of public officials if it turned into a radical state. The listing of target officials and power brokers would allow for quick regime *change if there was ever an unreasonable uprising of the Palestinian State.*

A couple years later, I later discussed this directly with the Assistant FBI on his vacation trip to Orlando, Florida... Not long after that there were some radical Palestinians targeted by U.S./Israel...

I disagreed with the hype and did a rare TV interview at http://thesop.org/politics/2006/07/31/harvey-carroll-jr-claims-to-have-had-a-hand-in-every-american-conflict-since-panama[10]

I sent in position papers to the CIA, and State Department. I then noticed President Bush, Jr. address the UN and recognize Palestine as a State.

---

[10] http://thesop.org/politics/2006/07/31/harvey-carroll-jr-claims-to-have-had-a-hand-in-every-american-conflict-since-panama *Rare TV interview discussing international affairs and my involvement...*

I can assure you that my position is very clear. I was against a return to Iraq for War and I think everyone sees now that I was right and the evidence shows that the war was unfounded. It knew that it would ultimately create more problems than it prevented.

In addition, analysts agree that it will inevitably create more terrorism in the long run. As well as cost trillions of dollars in direct and indirect cost, force economic down turns and more... Certainly putting America back into a deficit budget position and near bankruptcy like the collapse of the Soviet Union...

Here are some of my positions papers paraphrased and my attempt to prevent President George W. Bush from going to war with Iraq.

NOTE: I had a lot of papers, but I have decided to just paraphrase them in bullet form as not to largely repeat prior chapter so it flow smoothly and present the information quickly... We all know the issues by now, we as a nation now realize there were no Weapons of Mass Destructions (WMD's) found in Iraq, that there were no links to 9/11 Terrorist attack on the World Trade Center Twin Towers and the vast flawed intelligence.

- *I recognized the Joe 6 Pack of let's go kick ass and the statements of we should have gone on into Baghdad and finished the job the first time... Yet, that is easier said than done, and that those statements are just statements, uninformed and inexperienced opinions; and not a reason for war... (See 1ˢᵗ Gulf War Chapter).*

- *I refuted the intelligence that was being presented by Colin Powell, CIA Director Tenet, and the hype stirred up by CIA Agent Plum and her linking*

Iraq to the quest for Nuclear Weapons. I refuted the drum beating by National Security Advisor Condoleezza Rice.

- *I sent a large collection of letters, emails and position papers to President Bush, Vice President Cheney, the Senate, and Kentucky Senators, the State Department, CIA, the United Nations and the press related to National and International Policy related to Iraq and other current Diplomatic policy issues that might prevent war with Iraq... Here are letters from Senator Bunning and McConnell.*

JIM BUNNING
KENTUCKY

United States Senate
WASHINGTON, DC 20510

September 27, 2002

Mr. Harvey Carroll, Jr.
PO Box 657
Irvine, KY 40336-0657

Dear Mr. Carroll, Jr.:

Thank you for contacting me about the possibility of United States military action against Iraq. It is good to hear from you.

I agree with President Bush's repeated statements calling for an end to Saddam Hussein's brutal dictatorial regime in Iraq. Hussein's rule of Iraq has not only been detrimental to the welfare of the Iraqi people, but has also helped foster political instability in the Middle East. Our government has evidence that Hussein was involved in the 1993 bombing of the World Trade Center, and he attempted to assassinate former President George Bush. He is an obvious supporter of terrorism, as he also supports giving financial support to the families of radical suicide bombers that target innocent Israeli citizens. He directed his military to invade Iraq's neighbor - Kuwait, and he has even tested chemical weapons on the citizens of his own country. Since 1998, Hussein has not allowed United Nations arms and weapons inspectors into Iraq as stipulated in the treaty that ended the Gulf War. Every day more and more evidence is released that shows that Hussein continues to attempt to develop chemical, biological and nuclear weapons.

I am encouraged to hear there is a large number of Iraqis and Iraqi dissidents that also would like to see the end of Hussein's dictatorship. I am hopeful these pro-democracy and pro-human rights advocates can make some serious progress in weakening Hussein's brutal regime from within Iraq's borders. Should the United States attempt to overthrow Hussein, we must also remember we are attacking Hussein's regime and not the Iraqi people. A democratic regime change in Iraq would benefit not only the Iraqi people and the Middle East, but also the United States and the rest of the world.

Thank you for contacting me. Feel free to contact me at any time on any issue.

Best personal regards,

JIM BUNNING
United States Senator

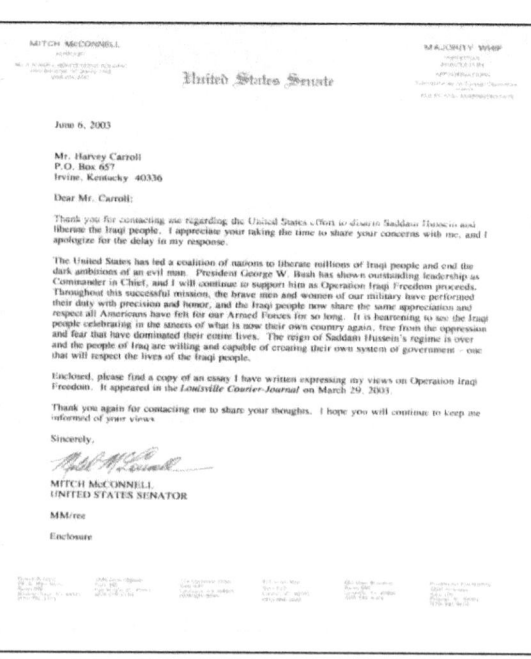

MITCH McCONNELL
KENTUCKY

MAJORITY WHIP

United States Senate

June 6, 2003

Mr. Harvey Carroll
P.O. Box 657
Irvine, Kentucky 40336

Dear Mr. Carroll:

Thank you for contacting me regarding the United States effort to disarm Saddam Hussein and liberate the Iraqi people. I appreciate your taking the time to share your concerns with me, and I apologize for the delay in my response.

The United States has led a coalition of nations to liberate millions of Iraqi people and end the dark ambitions of an evil man. President George W. Bush has shown outstanding leadership as Commander in Chief, and I will continue to support him as Operation Iraqi Freedom proceeds. Throughout this successful mission, the brave men and women of our military have performed their duty with precision and honor, and the Iraqi people now share the same appreciation and respect all Americans have felt for our Armed Forces for so long. It is heartening to see the Iraqi people celebrating in the streets of what is now their own country again, free from the oppression and fear that have dominated their entire lives. The reign of Saddam Hussein's regime is over and the people of Iraq are willing and capable of creating their own system of government - one that will respect the lives of the Iraqi people.

Enclosed, please find a copy of an essay I have written expressing my views on Operation Iraqi Freedom. It appeared in the *Louisville Courier-Journal* on March 29, 2003.

Thank you again for contacting me to share your thoughts. I hope you will continue to keep me informed of your views.

Sincerely,

MITCH McCONNELL
UNITED STATES SENATOR

MM/ree

Enclosure

You can see that both are ignoring sound intelligence. Both tow the Neo-Conservative line of faulty and fabricated intelligence links of Saddam Hussein being directly involved in World Trade Center bombings and try to infer 9/11 links to Iraq. Senator Bunning more particularly infers this. While Senator McConnell ignores getting back to me long after the war is started... Talk about ignoring intelligence and towing the rush to war line...

NOTE: Just by coincidence I'm watching C-SPAN coverage of a Congressional Hearing on Tuesday, December 29th, 2009 related to House Armed Service Subcommittee on Oversight. It is related to Military Strategic Education... I think I just found a market for this book... I just hope that they use it for the betterment and promotion of "Constructive Leadership as opposed to Destructive Leadership"...

I also hope that they promote peace for profit to maintain domestic and global growth and stable GDP to allow the military to receive a reasonable percentage of that GDP to maintain a focus on peace and prosperity....

TO often these war colleges fall in line and develop a reflective look of the Commander and Chief which is understandable line towing; however, there should be more emphasis on sound and reasonable intelligence positions to help develop policies of peace and prosperity as everyone gains with this mission statement/thesis...

Note: the following is a clutter of comments, letters, etc, but they went to relevant people in relevant places... All ignored sound intelligence and experience...

- *I presented a Federal Background Check and attempt to verify my credentials and experience too many relevant Government entities.*

- o *Granted the Federal Background Check was a bit on the wild side. Just going through and editing my book the past few days I can see why people have problems believing my claims; for I have done so much, been involved in so many issues, that it truly is beyond the average person's understanding.*

- o *With this said Senators and other public officials are in a position of frequently dealing with sensitive intelligence information and should have presented the views as viable alternatives if nothing more...*

- o *Yet, I presented a Federal Background Check that*

*validated my claims... To quote a Federal Investigator who was conducting a back ground investigation interview for one hour and forty-five minutes of being interviewed. "**That is the wildest story I've heard in thirty years as a federal investigator.**"*

NOTE: *I passed that Federal Background Investigation.*

- *I tried to share my background and experience with all the Hawkish war drummers that war is not fun and that it is serious... I know I have been there and that they didn't understand the complexities of the Middle East.*

- *I had dealt with PTSD for years after the Gulf War. I have lived, slept, eat and breathed Middle Easter Policy and Iraq Policy for decades and that the evidence they were presenting is faulty and will create more problems for America.*

- *I voiced that President Bush was running around destroying the coalition and not listening to former coalition partners and/or any voice of reason... But, we brought Russia in with us on the first Gulf war. How do I know this? Well, without getting into specific details and wording.*

- *I helped package a classified deal with Russia and the United States in order to get Russia to support our efforts during the 1st Gulf War. That deal was packaged at the Helsinki, Finland Summit between President Bush, Sr., and Russian President Gorbachev, that I suggested to be brokered by the Georgian President Edward Shevardnadze a trusted friend of both East and West.*

  - *That important deal included the United States providing*

Russia with millions of dollars to dismantle their deteriorating nuclear weapons and disposing of them in a secure fashion.

○ *I had foresight that such weapons of mass destruction could fall into the wrong hands "terrorist" years before the thought came to others minds having dealt with anti-terrorism in West Germany as an MP.*

○ *I sort of even had the foresight to anticipate an attack on the World Trade Centers by hijacking airlines in attempt to devastate this country economically for decades. Yet, I truly felt that such attacks would occur during a declared war time. I wasn't the only person that had anticipated such attacks. There was an investigator in Missouri that*

> *worked for the Governor that died in a place crash that had written papers on it... I had the website book marked at one time, but lost it in a computer crash and have not been able to find it since.*

- *I discussed the "First Strike Option"... At first I was sold by Colin Powell' UN address, but then my voice of reason kick in and I began to refute his statements.*

- *I tried to made it clear that Condoleezza Rice, and some CIA/Intelligence Agents had taking credit for much of my work with the Bush, Sr. Administrations 1st Gulf War and that they didn't have a clue of all the complexities and were not capable of entering Iraq as liberators.*

- *I considered myself a Diplomat by heart. I'm strongly for a UN resolution and encourage the "full" support of the UN to deal with Saddam in a constructive manner. But this does not justify war and I wrote the UN to voice this concern and to share the negative outcome for the world economy if it wasn't prevented.*

- *I called for the 2/15/03 UN Address of the UN/Senate to "admonish or fire" Powell/Tenet for lying to the UN stating that many careers have been built on my ability to analyze and deal with national and international affairs. My advice has helped Colin Powell improve his standing in the world and that I now wished to call attention that he was either misinformed and/or lying to the UN and Congress and presenting a false rush to war with Iraq.*

- *There was no shortage of case files that I worked on. I have a long standing track record of sending faxes to the White House, CIA, State Department in dealing with conflict and Diplomacy. Those writings have been very affective in packaging and implementing policy for a peaceful more prosperous world.*

- *I believed the UN Weapons Inspector Hans Blix who offered evidence that UN Security Council was being presented fabricating "fake photo's of trucks moving weapons." This is a very serious issue and I feel that the United States congress should admonish Secretary of State Powell/CIA Dir. George Tenet. Hans Blix noted in his address to the UN Security Council on February 14th 2003 that the photo's presented by Powell were "weeks not hours apart." This is a clear indication that Powell and Tenet were trying to push a sense of rush to conclusions (which I bought to be honest with you... I never expected Powell to lie in such a prestigious setting.) Therefore, he has lost a great deal of credibility with me.*

- *I agree with our European friends that Saddam is containable and that it is the right thing to do. There is so much more to this issue than the public knows. I would more than happily be willing to do huge press conference and discuss this for an hour or so if the Senate is willing to bring me to Washington for such a conference. I would also be willing to discuss this with the National Media...*

  - *I presented a draft UN Resolution that you can view on my link below and I repeat that I strongly feel Saddam is containable.*

- *He is also very strategically nukable. This extreme action could be done without destroying the world economy and plunging us into a lengthy world war.*

- *Lastly, I would like to thank the French for working so hard in trying to deal with this Diplomatically, the Germans for reminding us of their violent past and trying to share their empathy for us not to go down that evil path.*

8
DRAFT U.N. RESOULTION ON IRAQ TO COMPLY TO PREVENT WAR

I wrote all of the United Nations members with doubts that Iraq had WMD's per the Bush claims. I believed the U.N. Weapons Inspectors. So, I begin to try to influence the United Nations to be involved, but not militarily with a full invasion like the Bush camp was advocating...

Here are some of those thoughts...

1) *The US/UN will now vote as Proxy to the OPEC. It is suggested that the UN/US set up an Oil Ministry to be a voting member of OPEC in place of Iraq.*

2) *Establish an Iraqi Congress by splitting up Iraq into Congressional districts. By doing this the Shi'ites, Kurds and Sunnis would get a fair*

representative to voice their views and concerns.

3) Build a Wall around Israel... To pay for this I suggest the following:

- *Use a portion of the current aid going to the Middle East to build the wall. There is enough sand in the area to make concrete, so there shouldn't be a problem. In the process I suggest housing construction out of the same materials.*

- *Use a percentage of and Oil Fund from Iraq to pay for it. By doing this someday we will be able to communicate the fact that the Prophet Muhammad started the hate and should be able to reduce tensions to a coexistence level once that is realized and diminished.*

4) A permanent US/UN occupying force: This will be paid for by the following:

A) Set aside a percentage of Iraqi Oil to pay for the troops.

B) Continue to use funds that our budget allows.

C) Continue to use the funds that the UN Budget Allows.

5) Palestinian State: Plain and simple. Support the development of a Palestinian State as I have suggested in the Past and President Bush supported during his Previous UN Address. NOTE: I had sent the suggestion to State and CIA...

6) No Military Weapons of Mass Destruction and continued reduction of an Iraqi Military and put the citizens to work where they can thrive. The UN must continue to stay strong and supportive of the post-Gulf War and other UN Resolutions with no wavering

7) Establish and Economic Advisory

Board for the overseeing of Iraqi citizens economic wellbeing. Promote prosperity over a militaristic regime. Convert Iraq from a Destructive Economy to a Constructive Economy.

8) The most controversial issue of all is dealing with ███████████ *Through years of extensive research I've concluded that the* ███████████ *is the root of the destructive attitude and the author of the* ███████ *hate message directed towards Israel and others. We must establish a council to deal with the "Hate Message." Until we can deal with the fact that* ███████ *was the one that started (myarterism, the Jihad or Holy War against Israel; and that he was not a good role model in general then we can't have peace). I think we live in a time that people can recognize the human similarities and rise above one man's message of hate...*

My concerns for mankind:
As a last warning remember this.. I helped organize and maintain the multinational coalition in the 1st Gulf War. We all know that Iraq used chemical weapons in the Gulf War; hence, "Gulf War syndrome"... I'm sure this is a smoking gun for most people; however, it has been covered up for 12 years. So, should it really be a smoking gun.

Next the Gulf War cost a lot of lives and the destruction of over 600 oil wells with a war cost of about tens of Billion dollars. It affected our economy; Saudi's economy was nearly cut in half, possibly led to the Asian Crises and took money away from the reunification of Germany, the countries that participated side by side such as The UK and indirect cost to others throughout the world.

This time it will be much different. Saddam will be successful in bringing

Israel into the conflict the Arab coalition will turn against us. Unlike last time when I suggested Israel stay out. Our UN support is much less than before and much of the world is against us with an opinion that we are warmongers.

*Lastly, the cost of war vs the rewards. Iraq is estimated at having 6 Trillion in Oil Reserves. (You can check with DOE? This is not verified.) If it cost us 2 Trillion to take it, not to mention the economic loss sustained during a war time economy then were looking at about 3 or more trillion (**turned out to be trillions more and vastly affected the economy as I anticipated**). Then we have to take care of the citizens of Iraq to legitimize the liberation theory that we will attack on.*

Personally, my conscious without a huge defiance from Saddam would I support such destruction. So, I suggest we consider the positive solution to the war as I've outlined in the position paper above....

In general I was trying to get the U.N. to become a more permanent force with the cooperation of "Pizza Politics" in Iraq that could focus on "Comprehensive Planning" and a U.N. Peace force that maintains stability, not conflict...

9
REDNECKS RALLY TO "W" BUSH'S FALSE BILL OF GOODS TO RETURN TO IRAQ

Prior to the return to Iraq, I attended a pro-Bush/pro-war rally in Nashville, TN. Sponsored by Phil Valentine and John Bozeman. I had worked out an agreement to speak before the crowed to try to bring a voice of reason and justify why not to return to Iraq. So, I made the near 4 hour drive down to Nashville.

While at the rally that had been nationally promoted and hyped up there was only a turnout of about 2,000 people and the National Media.... The top country music stars that were rumored to attend and draw a crowd didn't even attend.

I got the impression that there aren't that many people for a war as President Bush is defining. This is evident in the heart of red neck country where we country boys will kick some ass at the drop of a hat and not think twice about   it.

Phil Valentine and company or should I say (Rush Limbaugh want to be) couldn't get a crowd any larger than some of my old college keg parties or small town street dances. Even with the rumor of top talent planning to attend. So, in my opinion his credibility is pretty much worthless in my book.

In fact, I pretty much left thinking "this guy is a joke." An event expecting 20 to 50 thousand only nets about 2 thousand...lol, lol. Yet, it was somewhat beneficial and reminded me even more how much President Bush is getting "terrible advice."

There are over 11 thousand IRAQI KURDS living in Nashville, TN. Area. With such a large population they have key community leaders that gave speeches. Sure, they were pro American and regurgitated the same old Saddam is a blanked, blank, blank.....

As I discussed potential policy with the KURD representatives and members of the Kurdish Human Rights Watch (Isa Tayip .... and Saeed Chalky we came to the same conclusions that Bush had terrible strategy in trying to bring in Turkey over the Kurds.

There are over 6 million Kurds with about a 70 thousand man Army. Even though, Isa felt that the Kurds could take Baghdad in 3 days I doubted it and felt that they would have done it years ago if they could have. He did have a legitimate concern that they would *have done much better if they could stop Iraqi air strikes on their attempts.*

I felt that if anything the United States should work with the Kurds to take the North Oil Fields in Iraq just as the US would freeze any terrorist assets held by banks in the United States.

By taking their money it limits their ability to finance their terror operations. So, perhaps the Kurds and the United States air support could draw a line in the sand somewhere around the Northern no fly zone to protect the Kurds and help them take over and secure the Northern Iraqi Oil Fields. Potential strategy could be organized with the Shi'ites and Sunnis in the Southern Iraqi areas. "Pizza Politics" of dividing Iraq into three parts would have prevented Civil Conflict and a U.S. return...

10
BUILDING A WALL AROUND ISRAEL AND PEACE PARK

Democracy, Diplomacy and Development in the Middle East, I feel to be of key priority to establish Peace in the Middle East. Diplomacy, with citizens involved in progressive democracy and development is constructive and not destructive.

In addition, we should define the concept of realism in that "The United States has a critical role to play in helping out".[11] It may be good to start with this public discussion, because, Small[12] suggest that it takes about one and a half years before an initiative can be go on record as policy. Therefore, we need to go to the United Nations and

---

[11] Thomas Carothers, <u>4 Reasons to Aid Democracy Abroad,</u> <wysiwyg://1/http://washingtonpost.com/wp-dyn/articles/A59855-2001Jan29.html>

[12] Melvin Small, <u>Democracy and Diplomacy: The Impact of Domestic Politics on U.S. Foreign Policy</u> (Baltimore: The Johns Hopkins University Press, 1996) Intro. Pg. xii.

voice our leadership and quest for cooperation in creating a more peaceful and prospers world... A world that values the United Nations Declaration of Human Rights and the responsibilities to focus on promoting international trade and commerce...

Our policy makers will need to realize that there will be opponents against democracy who will also claim to be "REALIST"; therefore, it is imperative to stress constructive policies over destructive ones.

Such opposition will use dialog similar to if not from the writings of Layne[13] whom we shut down the structural argument; however, we will need to consider a serious look at crises behavior.

---

[13] Class notes and Dr. Desches summation of Michael E. Brown, et. Al, <u>Debating the Democratic Peace (An International Security Reader</u>, (Cambridge: MIT Press 1996). Layne Chapters.

Other opponents such as Farber and Gowa[14] argue against a democratic peace and pages of skewed worthless data that is supposed to represent the democratic statistical analysis of Spiro;[15] whom claims there is no statistical evidence to say that democracy promotes peace any more than any other kind of government.

However, I disagree with the opponents to democracy and their definition of a "REALIST". Reality is what people believe to be real and if there is an overwhelming consensus that democracy promotes peace then it will be a constructive tool and meet people's expectations for the promotion of a democratic peace and prosperity... After all the United Nations is a Democratic forum where they can adopt and pass a

---

[14] Michael E. Brown, et. Al, <u>Debating the Democratic Peace (An International Security Reader</u>, (Cambridge: MIT Press 1996). Spiro Chapters.

[15] Michael E. Brown, et. Al<u>, Debating the Democratic Peace (An International Security Reader</u>, (Cambridge: MIT Press 1996). Spiro Chapter.

new focus on a lasting "1,000 year peace and prosperity plan" if they chose to do so.... With respect to those ends, I feel that President Obama can and should continue the role of promoting democracy in the following areas:

America and the U.N. must continue having a presence in the Middle East and the promotion and recognition of the various Arab and Persian states and their quest for honest Democracies. Prime recognition must go to Palestine as a State and foremost is the need for a "Co-Existence Zone" between Palestine and Israel.

I will discuss this in more detail further in this chapter because it is imperative for Middle Eastern Peace, the safety and promotion of tourism for a more peaceful and prosperous region...

The M.E. must try to ensure that it is in transition to a constitutional democracy cited in earlier chapters. American needs to quit being the 800 lb. gorilla pushing our weight around and quite trying to delegitimize Middle East Political Elections as we have in Iran.

We should focus on diplomacy and development, via sound "Comprehensive Planning"[16] instead of spending ½ Trillion a year on Middle Eastern Defense...

This vast yearly spending came at a price of nearly 10 Trillion spent on Middle Eastern conflict and the worst economic downturn since the Great Depression. All of the cost could-have

---

[16] Comprehensive Planning tool to be used for economic development
https://spreadsheets.google.com/ccc?key=0AuygIxNdW7E9dFlrS3VOWmgwbXJwQWNNOVpaNzBPckE&hl=en&authkey=CKKqj5gP

been avoided if we had not returned to Iraq, but since we did go there, I feel that most of the cost could have been avoided if we had not missed the opportunity to cut Iraq into slices like a Pizza.

Pizza Politics would have saved America nearly 10 Trillion Dollars and gained support from the neighboring countries around Iraq as they got a diminished threat of Nationalism and established DMZ Buffer Zone between other neighbors... This strategy could have also divided nationalism and separated sectarian violence...

*That along with the Nuclear Free/Co-Existence Zone and the development of the "**Wall of Restitution**", whereby, Oil revenues will be used to expand the wall between Israel and the Palestinian State, and convert the Wall into Town Homes instead of razor wire and land mines. This will go* *hand in hand with a "Comprehensive Plan"[17] for Democracy and Development of the infant democracy states of Palestine and Israel.*

Bible Verbatim text:[18]

"1 I looked up and saw a man with a measuring line in his hand. 2 I asked him, "Where are you going?" He answered, "I am going to measure Jerusalem to see how wide and how long it is." 3 Then the angel who was speaking with me left. Another angel came out to meet him 4 and said to him, "Run, and say to that young man, 'Jerusalem will be inhabited like an un-walled village because it will

---

[17] Comprehensive Planning tool to be used for economic development
https://spreadsheets.google.com/ccc?key=0AuygIxNdW7E9dFlrS3VOWmgwbXJwQWNNOVpaNzBPckE&hl=en&authkey=CKKqj5gP

[18] GOD'S WORD is a copyrighted work of God's Word to the Nations. Quotations are used by permission.
Copyright 1995 by God's Word to the Nations. All rights reserved. http://www.godsword.org/

have so many people and animals in it. 5 I will be a wall of fire around it, declares the LORD. I will be the glory within it."

Summing this up we as men should not set the boundaries, for it is God who will set the boundaries of Israel, and all other nations; however, men are leading the countries and they have to be respondent to their people's needs.

I honestly and justly just feel this is a way for men to respond to housing needs and create a Co-Existence Zone of Peace in the process... There a way to make the wall and/or boundaries in the form of town homes and condos that benefit all nations in the region; perhaps this economic development wall will continue around the world and perhaps even someday connect into the Great Wall of China; thereby, building homes/flats along that wall as well...

Israel and "Peace Park"-- I feel that "PEACE PARK" can solve the "Two State Solution Problems" and still provide new housing for both states...

Many great Theme Parks in the world attract millions of visitors each and every year. These amazing theme parks also bring tens of thousands of jobs, and successful economic development to those communities.

With this in mind, I am proposing that a Co-Existence Zone be agreed upon between Israel and Palestine to develop "PEACE PARK"; whereby, there will be true peace and prosperity within the Middle East between the two States of Israel and Palestine.

PEACE PARK would attract the support and cooperation of Engineers, Builders, Investors/Land Developers, and Capital Markets from around the world. As the park becomes a success, it will bring millions from around the world. In turn those multitudes will bring trade and commerce opportunities that will feed, clothe and shelter those within the Middle East.

PEACE PARK may still have a wall in key areas; however, this wall should be built in the form of TOWN HOMES, FLATS, AND COMMERCIAL, RETAIL, HOTEL, AND OFFICE strips...

One state on one side and the other on the other side... These Town Homes can run for miles upon miles to create a border; however, provide beautiful and safe communities. Communities complete with well-constructed housing, courtyards, gardens and other green space, and wonderful promenades with old world street lighting to light the path to PEACE PARK.

I hope to hear and see large peaceful rallies calling for PEACE PARK within the Co-existence Zone calling for a safe and secure place for all families, and children to be able to live and play in peace...

PEACE PARK could be built in Cashmere and other viable hot spots within the world. In fact, I have already discussed the issue with key political groups in the area and they are interested in promoting it...

11
THE FED, THE COMMISSONED CONGRESS AND "W" BUSHES "MONEY CHANGERS"

America's national debt just went over 19 Trillion Dollars, this is not good WWW.USDEBTCLOCK.ORG.

We as a nation have to realize that the debt increase is related to an American Common Defense that has lost its commonsense.

We also have to realize as a nation that the FED policies that influenced the subprime housing policies were directly related to the Bush War-Time Economy. In order to stimulate the War-Time Economy the FED lowered rates. Lower interest rates had an inverse relationship that increased inflation values of homes. This continued as speculators saw a 15 to 20% increases in values in some areas such as Florida. They felt they could buy and in 5 years double their money... Most of the nation was riding the wave of inflation, but that wave his the American economy like a tsunami...

That tsunami destroyed the American Dream of home ownership for millions of Americas, with values dropping about 40% nationwide. This vast mismanagement from the White House, Congress and the FED created the problem, not the American homebuyer... So stop blaming them...

I had often defended the FED, while many wished to condemn the Federal Reserve Banking System (FED). The FED was not without its problems; however, all throughout history there have always been faults with money and banking. Yet, with all of money and banking faults, Civil Society needs a form of money and banking. We just have to focus on constructive leadership that enhances as opposed to destroying the value... "In God We Trust" wasn't put on our paper money for nothing... With faith we can return to a constructive and prosperous society...

I see that many of the same problems that existed 2000 years ago when Christ threw the money-changers out of the Temple. Christ was very upset with the lack of respect for the Temple/Church, as it was not a place of business. The Temple/Church was in the business of saving souls and helping improve the minds and goodness of humanity. Money-changers had their purpose, just as the FED of today has its purpose.

There is a need for FED Reforms, which could make things easier for the multitudes. Money and banking is a viable need. We just have to focus on "Comprehensive Planning" to revitalize the American and Global Economy...

Being inside the Temple doing business was as rude as having a loud cell phone conversation in Church or a Movie today. It was just not appropriate, nor is it appropriate today for profiteers to invoke God`s name to perpetrate conflicts for profit. So, how can we solve these problems?

I feel that too many Christians and politicians and the like try to associate the anger Christ had with the money-changers to that of Wall Street, Banks, and the Federal Reserve System that maintains the global economic system. Yet, it is fair to hold them to standards and keep them out of the Temple and interfering with the sanctity of humanity...

For far too long the "Money Changes" of Wall Street and Washington have led a demonic defense policy that has undermined the American Dream and nearly destroyed the Global

Economy.

Bad fiscal policy making has caused America and Christians to fall behind in many respects. Without money it has been hard to do Gods great deeds around the world. Or perhaps this is why In God We Trust was printed upon American money.

My question is how can we print more, and do more to educate and improve humanity for good as opposed to evil? We must start by being a constructive example; this will require change, a lot of change in the way we have become over the past decade and a half.

People feel that there will be no changes in the FED in the near point in history, and it will continue to point to the American Federal Reserve System and other Central Banks around the world as being the modern day moneychangers and the root of all evil, but I disagree.

I recognize the value of the FED as all throughout history there had been the rise and fall of economies. The Federal Reserve System in many ways was a 4th Branch of Government, which could cause the rise and fall of a nation...

Big Business special interest and the "War Time Economy" has been the 4th Branch of Government for too long. The FED must reform as should Washington, to adhere to the founding fathers rules of Checks and Balance.

America must focus on constructive use of the FED as opposed to going more deeply into debt with little return on investments...

I and others have argued all throughout history to prevent money and banking, Central Banks, or FED and its equivalent of money-changers within the Temple to encourage and/or via special interest funding buy Government into running up debt and engaging in War for profit.

As central banks increase debt, and feed the money-changers thirst for blood and power they benefit the few special interest entities within their fold.

The industries that they control as well as the interest created out of thin air. Those industries serve to benefit the few hands that wealth was shifted into via interest on debt to money-changers, and those that feed upon Americas blood and treasure...

The only way to change this is via a long-term education plans. Yet, we must offer far more value to both the "Money Changers" and to Humanity at the same time... This will require the creation of a more serious

"Comprehensive Planning" and development program to revitalize America and the world.

I believe that in order to survive the human race must have an American Common Defense that has commonsense. We must have a Defense Industry that does not cater to special interest. Nor should a FED or Commissioned Congress serve the interest of a few over America and humanities best interest...

There are ideas out in the World that visualize a "New Earth Army" and I believe in that plan. A "New Earth Army" could do humanitarian interventions like in Somalia, Libya and Syria with limited and/or without engagement... They could focus on dividing warring factions, and focusing more on allowing time for sound diplomacy, democracy, and development

I often note that many great economies throughout history story have risen and fell via poor management of their citizens, and their nation's great wealth.

I would like to see a form of stability, and regulation in the markets that will protect investor's funds. However, I do not advocate for the ending of the Federal Reserve System (The FED).

I believe in the soundless of paper money over that of the Gold Standard, which is those with the gold rules. I'm more in line with the Bible's Golden Rule "Do unto others as you would have others do unto you." We can do this via "Comprehensive Planning" in every community, city and state by working together to develop a Golden Civil Society...

I like to be constructive and

forward thinking. It's important for the World and Americans to again see opportunities. America and the World is huge and millions of years of future growth and development. It only requires a serious focus on comprehensive planning, which is the real form of money...

Seriously, "Revitalization" via "Comprehensive Planning" is the real form of money is providing services to help supply the needs and wants of humanity in our communities, cities and nations... And let's do that in a constructive way...

It's crazy to think that I had also suggested former Soviet States. And even again financial AID via the IFC/World Bank for Ukraine that saved seventy-five banks a few years ago. Helping former Communist bloc countries that were once enemies, now the entire country of Ukraine can be a

103

University to educate in culture, economics and language exchange between the East and West to further humanity.

Or it can fall from a buffer zone state into a Proxy Conflict between the West and Russia due to paranoid policies of the past... Currently, it could quickly go either way... But, I have done what I could to focus on the more constructive route...

I shared a similar "Bailout Plans" with the U.S. House and Senate Financial Services Committee "Frank and Dodd." It was required to bailout the American Economy. Nearly 2/3rds of the American States and Top Banks were near Soviet Union type Collapse...

Lessons I learned by integrating myself into the former Soviet Culture by visiting Ukraine kept America from going the same route to collapse. Yet, if we do not make major changes soon we will fall and take the entire Global economy with us...

12
REVITIALIZING AMERICA
AND THE GLOBAL ECONOMY
VIA "COMPREHENSIVE PLANNING"

We must act now in every community, city, state and nation to focus on "Comprehensive Planning," because the World is in a very difficult situation... There is great urgency to act now for an American and United Nations Global Reform Mandate to revitalize the American and Global Economy.

I urge caution as the past has shown that when many central banks begin to have problems, and more and more citizens begin to feel the stresses and depression, that wars often follow.

The vast death and destruction of two World Wars, and a number of others major conflicts, humanity should have learned its lesson. We must try to avoid returning down the bloody paths of the past.

I strongly feel that America and the world is in need of more dreamers, those with real vivid dreams and visions that offer up constructive leadership. People offer such bold projects of the past, like the TVA, Hoover Dam, the Continental Rail Road, the Federal Highway System and the like to get America motivated and off their ass to make great things happen. I recognize that America is still young and virtually undeveloped; it is up to you and your decedents to make America great...

I feel that America needs to revitalize its education via funding my like my KERA (Kentucky Education Reform Act), perhaps you will read my book on it also.

I strongly feel that America needs a School "Dress Code" to focus more on education than what one wears to class.

America also needs more constructive mentoring programs. American can gain youthful leadership experience. These are important so that they can learn visualize and share new and bold visions for America and the world.

I see America as needing to get on the path to prosperity, and feels that America can look to the future, and to the heavens with faith, builds new paths/roads and passenger and freight rail systems throughout America, process timbers into lumber, furniture, and homes to live the American Dream.

Americans can move mountains, mine the minerals, clear great roadbeds to build roads, and railroads, build bridges. Americans can invest internally and gain national and international investors

Community Reinvestment and FDI put

into honest and profitable *"Comprehensive Planning"* PPP' projects are very important. Planning is the only way to stabilize America and the Global economy.

A focus on quality reinvestments in our communities, cities, states and throughout America is necessary. Comprehensive Planning can ramp up new and expanding factories in affordable communities...

International Trade The market is down; however, VAT subsidized focus on refining petroleum, and natural gas.

There is an obvious need to, build new forms of transportation and mass transit, and build new, sustainable, and very environmentally friendly green energy to supply those new and expanding communities along the way.

I thought I would put this last part

of the chapter in more of an outline form to point out key aspects of Revitalizing America...

***America is Great**; it will be up to America to decide if you need Trump or not.*

I can tell you America need people make revitalize America.

NOTE: In 2000 I ran for President. Some of Trump's people ask me if I would consider running with him. I was flattered, but I turned them down to focus on my own run. First and foremost,

I thought Trump as a business man had earned respect, but he had not paid his dues as I had in the political arena. Yet, later as Pat Buchannan became the front runner I wrote him and reconsidered... Perhaps a story for another day...

December 14, 1999

Harvey Carroll, Jr.
806 Brockton
Richmond, KY 40475

Dear Mr. Carroll,

Mr. Trump appreciates your offer to join him as the Vice Presidential candidate in the 2000 election. Currently, he is seriously considering a bid for the Reform Party Presidential nomination and will make a decision early next year. Since he is not a declared candidate for the Presidency at this time, it is simply too early for him to consider possible running mates.

He believes the Republicans have gone too far to the Right. The Democrats have gone too far to the Left. Mr. Trump thinks the Reform Party could offer the citizens of our country the best opportunity to address the needs of the working men and women in the center.

It is time for the United States to have a leader who can break the logjam in Washington. Americans need that leader to negotiate real tax relief and reform our healthcare, social security and campaign finance systems.

Mr. Trump agrees with you that our next President must be someone who sees the big picture and is not beholden to special interests. Perhaps America is ready to have an experienced businessman who will run America like a business at the helm.

Your support is greatly appreciated.

Sincerely,

Roger Stone, Director
Donald J. Trump Presidential Exploratory Committee

Trump Tower 725 Fifth Avenue 15th Floor New York, NY 10022 212.688.7230 (TEL) 212 688 4020 (FAX)
www.DonaldJTrump2000.com

NOTE: You will find that Trump's 10 Billion Dollar Empire from running a few businesses and Atlantic City Gambling is like a drop in the bucket to the vast accomplishments that I have achieved for America and humanity...

Some key points to keep in mind for Revitalizing America:

- *America has a great Constitution, written over 200 years ago by our Founding Fathers, which still guide us today.*
- *America has the largest economy in the world...*
- *America has the best roads, small business, and job base, as well as the best educational institutions in the world.*
- *****Yet, all need revitalized...*

My reputation and credibility will become more and more known in the coming months, and I can assure you that I'm telling the truth that America is already Great, but it is up to the American people "you" to revitalize America...)

My reputation and credibility will

show you the history of a man, not of vast wealth, but wisdom. The wisdom to consult God with tough decisions, the wisdom to have faith that I can go far beyond my limitations; faith that has saved millions of lives, and affected the economic fate of America and many other nations.

America Needs...

Yes, America is in very bad need of "Revitalization," but it does not need to be made great again, because America is great; however, America and American's are not living up to our fullest potential.

- *We need to "Revitalize" our communities, cities and states via "Comprehensive Planning."*
- *There are a number of "Comprehensive Plans" that are available today, often free from other cities; I have a 25 page template that can easily be followed to "Revitalize" all of America, and to create vast*

growth and development.

- *This simple to use template "Comprehensive Plan" template will grow our communities, grow our cities, and grow the American economy to aid in our Economic National Security and the use of our valued Economic Statecraft Influence throughout the World.*

  - *No more "Bullshit Artist" we need real Professional Public Administrators working with elected City Officials, inviting Civil Society Groups to assess needs and wants, and then working with Business via Public-Private-Partnerships to plan, organize, implement and control the budgets to maximize growth and development. This is real Revitalization and showing the Greatness of America...*

<u>Education Revitalization</u> *should begin with "America-Dress for Success-Dress*

Code" in our schools and universities as the standard to get our focus back on learning priorities.

- *Decades ago I helped Kentucky Governor Wilkinson package and sell KERA (Kentucky Education Reform Act) that created multibillion dollar educational funding for Kentucky; we must invest from our states and nation... (Trump got where he is because of an expensive and quality business education, such education should be made more affordable to more people.)*
- *A "Penny for our Thoughts" and other funding focus can get America back on the path of being the best funded Educational resource leader in the World; you must be aware that others wish to cut State and Federal Educational funding...*
- *In the 1970's America was the leading Educational provider in the World. Now, we are on a downhill slope, we must get back on the lift and raise our*

standards of education...

- "America-Dress for Success-Dress Code", funding focus, and remembering that we were once the leaders in the 1970's in Global Education can revitalize America's Education system...

Welfare, Comprehensive Planning and Debt Reduction, International Trade and Commerce Revitalization.

America has had vast Job losses. Welfare went from 17 to 45 million, and poverty reached nearly 80 million Americans. We must stop this trend, by creating jobs.

- Comprehensive Planning, a VAT on Imports to create a "Fair Trade" as opposed to Free Trade that cost America nearly 1 Trillion a year and export our jobs must be a priority...
- Debt Reduction is one of the most serious issues facing

Americas National Security...

- *Economic Security, be it with our jobs, homes, and businesses or our cities, states, and nations debt; Americans must budget wisely...*

- *Since 2000 the National Debt climbed from a bit over 4 Trillion to nearly 20 Trillion Dollars that is placing America at a near Soviet Union type economic collapse; yet, we can prevent it via "Comprehensive Planning" a focus on debt management and reduction, a strong focus on improving our Trade Deals...*

- *Reagan got it right with "Supply Side Economics" vs the Bush/McConnell concepts of "Buy Side Economics".*

- *America has a near 1 Trillion a year Trade imbalance that exports our Jobs overseas, as opposed to our products made in the USA.*

  - *We must manage our Trade and Tariffs' not via isolation or protectionism, but through "Fair Trade" as opposed to "Free Trade" that is costing America 1 trillion a year; "There is nothing free about Free Trade."*

America must create jobs to reduce Welfare, and America must reduce its 1 Trillion a year Trade Imbalance, by improving our Trade and Commerce to reduce our Trade Imbalance...

<u>Diplomacy and Defense Policy</u>
"Americas Common Defense has lost its Commonsense."

I have one of the best "Defense" background in the World.

- *I have dealt with the Panama Invasion, helped plan, organize and maintain the successful multinational coalition during "Desert Storm" (the 100 hour war-4 days, 4 hours, as opposed to dilly dallying around in the desert for a decade like the Bush/Cheney return to Iraq).*

- *I made the suggestion for the Military Mission to Somalia that got turned into a Military Mission with Defense with no Commonsense.*

- *I made the suggestion for "Humanitarian Intervention" into Libya.*

- *Suggestions to reduce conflict while in Ukraine, as well as bailouts and assistance that kept nuclear weapons off the black markets post-Soviet Collapse...*

- *Panama, 1st Gulf War, Somalia, Middle East, Ukraine/Russia post-Soviet Collapse nuclear buyout, and more, much more...*

- *I've seen first-hand where Defense with little Commonsense had more influence than Diplomacy with vast Commonsense...*

- *Diplomacy must have its chance to work...*
- *Diplomacy along with Economic Statecraft can prevent vast death and destruction, and the crippling of the American, and Global Economy.*
- *Like Americas vast Trade Imbalance our Common Defense went from a bit over 300 billion to nearly 1 Trillion a year during the Bush/Cheney era.*
- *This horrific squandering continued to increase in the debt ceiling, while reducing the overall Defense Budget that now goes to China to pay off debts instead of keeping America secure...*
- *The near 2.2 Billion a day Defense Budget of War in the Middle East, while importing 12 to 18 times less oil per day made*

no reasonable sense, and certainly no economic commonsense...

- *I feel that my reputation and credibility as a "Commander n Chief" type man is second to none.*

- *I've seen America's Common Defense, with little to no commonsense; has undermined America's entire Economic National Security, while not giving Diplomacy and American Economic Statecraft more chances to prevent conflict.*

- *I've also watched the Defense Budget nearly destroy the Economic National Security interest of the United States, while providing a fraction in return; thereby, not justifying the "Use of Force" in returning to Middle Eastern Conflicts...*

NOTE: This alone far exceeds the

expectations of any of the Presidential hopefuls in the 2016 race... But, it is up to America to recognize this, and to share in providing leadership, as opposed to messages of hate, or return to failed policies, with more of the same economic national security failures that has placing America in a near Soviet Collapse situation...

"The American Dream" should be restored...

Outside of the inner circle of "Beltway Bandits" no one is happy with the Political Policy Making in Washington since about 2000.

- Americans have lost the dream, been screwed, drugged up and tattooed...

- We must change the paths were on, or we will not survive as a Nation, nor will Humanity progress...

- We must reverse our foundation of fear, and return to the foundation *of our founding fathers "Bill of Rights" not just for Americans, but offer this great bill of rights to all humanity to include ISIS.*

- *Simple freedoms go a long way in changing ideologies.*

- *Freedom has won great Wars, brought down the Iron Curtain that led to the largest expansion of freedom in history.*
- *Such freedoms can do far more to reduce terrorism than dropping blind bombs that kill the innocent...*
- *According to History we see "Freedoms" have always outweighed Fascism and false ideological foundations.*

It's true! You can find dozens of accounts in our history books, or throughout the Bible, and/or other religious text...

A focus on Freedoms "Bill of Rights"

and "Comprehensive Planning" for Terror stricken regions can lead to a reduction of Terrorism.

- *Drone strike that kills someone's child--this only makes a potential Terrorist out of a parent.*
- *An Air Strike that kills parents--this only makes a potential Terrorist out of a young child that has lost a parent.*
- *Allowing conflict that cause millions to lose everything—this only makes a potential Terrorist out of anyone that faces the West's failed Policies...*
- *Using American "Bill of Rights" values and commonsense as opposed to American common defense without commonsense is truly the answer to reducing terrorism, and the path to peace in the Middle East and around the World...*

America needs vision and leadership..

A. Imagine yourself thinking of how

you could use the "Golden Rule" that we have come to know children. "Do unto others as you would have others do unto you."

- *You would not want your children droned.*
- *You would not want to hold your dead child in your arms.*
- *You would not want to see and hear Western press reporting drone strikes to be successful and knowing that your child was not a terrorist.*
- *You would not want your parent Air Struck.*
- *You would not want your parents droned.*
- *You would not want to hold your dead parents in your arms.*
- *You would not want to see and hear Western press reporting drone strikes to be successful and knowing that your parents were not terrorists.*

B. And you certainly would not want to

lose everything you owned.

- *You would not want to walk thousands of miles to areas that believe you to be a terrorist.*
- *You would not want to begin thinking why you shouldn't be a terrorist since you are no longer treated like a human being.*
- *But, would you, especially after you have lost everything because of the western policies failed to provide constructive leadership...*
- *We have to look little farther than our school shootings to see that American tempers are even far less tolerating than those that are experiencing real losses, real hardships, and real abuse...*

I have empathy for those feeling the war

zones that have lost everything, they are strong and tolerant; I strongly feel that Americans can learn from their tolerance...

The Actions that America needs to take.

Summary of problems is a long list, but there are a few key items that can revitalize America...

- *Realize I have vast credibility, capabilities and have to focus on a long term commitment to constructive policy making.*
- *We must focus on revitalizing America via "Comprehensive Planning" in every community, city, state, and lead in revitalizing America and the Global economy...*
- *America must reduce its near Trillion Dollar a year Trade Imbalance and reduce its debt. A VAT can assist with both...*
- *We must focus on Welfare*

reduction that climbed from 17 to 45 million Americans since the Bush economy... Workfare must be a focus.

- *Educational reforms "Penny for your Thoughts" along with "Dress Codes" to revitalize America's educational system must be our priority... We must find a way to educate 3 for the price of one... I call upon educational institutions to make it happen...*
  - *Call all American's to Immediate Action...*
- *I call upon Congress to sign a "No-Commission" pledge to reduce corrupt lobbying.*
- *I call for the Press to begin "Oversight Investigations" on the true squandering of Trillions of dollars from American Common Defense that has lost its commonsense since the return to Iraq...*
- *I call upon Citizens of the World to*

look to a future of greatness and not that of becoming a demonic terrorist... Have patients and tolerance and believe in the basic "Bill of Rights" that we as Americans value and make them your own instead of embracing terror...

- *I call upon every community leader, city official, state official and nation to begin looking at "Comprehensive Planning" at all levels to revitalize growth and development, this and only this will bring America and the World out of economic despair...*
- *I call for educational institution to make 3 for the price of 1 a reality, and try to go even further in reducing educational cost; especially, in Small Business, as well as implement Professional Public Administration Programs that can revitalize America...*
  - *I call upon Congress and the*

United States Department of Commerce to begin looking at workable VAT's to reduce the near 1 Trillion a year Trade Imbalance, and how the VAT can also help reduce the deficit.

Remember, we are judged on earth and heaven by our words and deeds... It is time to be judged...

Conclusions:

I hope that you realize the difficulties that I dealt with during the 1st Gulf War, opposing and seeing the Bush blunders during the return to Iraq. Then those of you that have had to deal with PTSD know that dealing with war isn't too easy.

Readers should question their leaders. Those that are rallying for defense and policies that can lead to war have to be scrutinized. Talking tough can lead to huge problems. Bush talked touch during his near two year campaign... The Axis of Evil got stronger...

Use commonsense. For example, if you were in a bar and some loud mouth began trying to start a fight, are you going to be eager to join him? No, then why would you an American want to follow leaders that are being the drunk in the bar?

Sure, there is a time to fight, but be the guy that is sitting quite, watching the game, having a meal and is being bullied... Backed into a corner where you are left with no other options but to fight... But, even then try Diplomacy...

I've earned the right to say that American common Defense has lost its commonsense. We as a nation need to begin looking at bringing the military back to civilian control. Civil Societies resources are being squandered while the American people were sold a false bill of goods...

This has been true all throughout history. Many great nations rose and fell because of paranoid defense policies. We must recognize that our own paranoid policies of the past have placed us in economic national security risk, as well as on the fast track for cultural decline, lack of educational focus and much more...

We must cut the Defense fat; hone it to readiness and rapid deployment. Yet, we must make it a "New Earth's Army" that works closely with the 3D's of Democracy, Diplomacy and Development.

We need to focus more on international trade and commerce that is balanced with fair trade that will improve our GDP. More focus at the city, state and national "Comprehensive Planning" to create the needed growth and development to improve our overall America's GDP demands...

My "Operation Desert Storm"
My suggestions for the 1st Gulf War
(The 100 Hour War)
(THE UNELECTED PRESIDENT)
By
Harvey Carroll, Jr.

I'm a former U.S. Army Military Policeman/Investigator, whom took an "International Relations and U.S. Foreign Policy" class while in the Army in 1985. That class led to preventing WWIII in the Middle East and my helping to organize the multinational coalition during the 1st Gulf War "Operation Desert Storm."

I now hold a Bachelors of Business Administration Degree specializing in Real Estate and Finance, and three partial Masters in Business, Public Administration as well as Diplomacy and International Commerce...

I've been considered the most influential international political figure in Kentucky-US, and some would say that perhaps in the World at one time. I have dealt with Governors, Senators, Presidents and Foreign Heads of State; and in the process I have saved millions of lives, and affected the economic fate of nations... Yet, I have made mistakes, and even cost lives and often ponder if the "End Justified the Means."

It has always been quite easy for me to deal with complex U.S. National and International Policy. From a young age I dealt with local, state, national and international policy that includes Latin America i.e. "Panama," Middle East (Iraq, Libya, Syria, Israel, Iran), Africa, and even coming to the AID after the collapse of the Soviet Union to protect U.S. and Global Security by suggesting buying out the nuclear weapons to prevent them from ending up on the Black Market for Terrorism, as well as preventing the former fifteen Soviet States against each other.

I also suggested financial bailouts, and another financial AID via the IFC/World Bank for Ukraine that saved seventy-five banks a few years ago (a similar plan presented to the U.S. House and Senate Financial Services Committee "Frank and Dodd" to bailout the American Economy to assist 2/3rds of the American States and Top Banks from Collapse.

More recently, I have shared suggestions to have the OSCE get between the separatist and the Ukrainian Army to the Ukrainian Presidents people tasked to negotiate the Minsk Agreements that may have prevented Ukraine from turning into another Syria... In the process I have noticed that Russian President Putin sent Troops "Little Green Men" into Crimea; thereby, I responded by sharing "Peace Negotiations" and a "Crimean Compromise"...